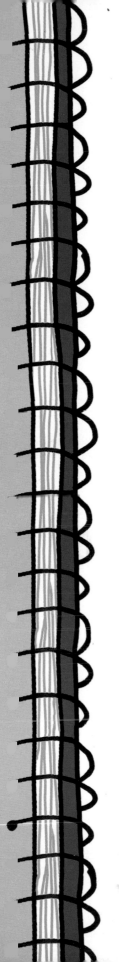

Last week, Peter and I got a new kitten. His name is George, and he's adorable! We were having a great time playing chase the mouse with him today – until Dad came in.

"You two need to do your jobs, now," he said.

"I don't want to," Peter whined.

"Come on," I said to Peter. "We'll make it fun."

"Fun jobs?" Peter exclaimed. "Have you ever heard of fun jobs, George?"

George made a cute little purring sound.

"I didn't think so," Peter answered.

"I've been studying simple machines," I told Peter. "They can help us with the work."

"How about a simple machine that simply does all the work for us?" Peter asked.

"That would not be a simple machine," I explained. "A simple machine is much more, well, simple. It's a fundamental tool that helps you do work."

"There's that word again," Peter said.

"What word?" I asked.

"Fun," he said. "Fun-da-pimple."

"Fundamental," I said. "It means it's really basic. It has few or no moving parts. Simple machines are everywhere! You probably use them all the time and don't even know it." I grabbed my trusty science notebook to write down all the different types of simple machines.

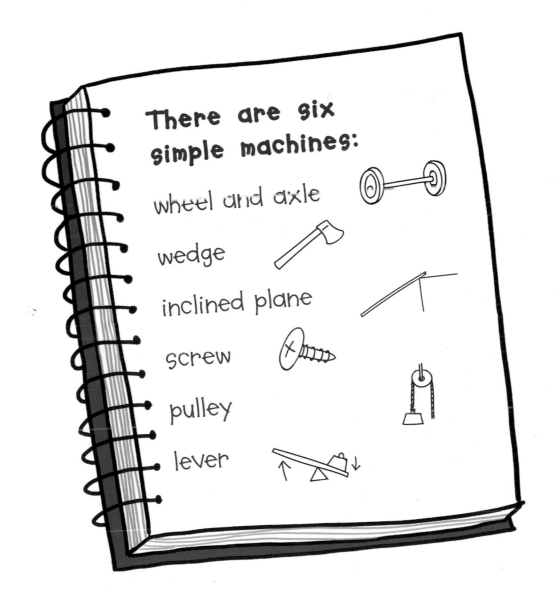

There are six simple machines:

wheel and axle

wedge

inclined plane

screw

pulley

lever

Our first job was to pick up Peter's toys. They were all over the house. He keeps them in a big box, but the box gets heavy when you put a lot of toys in it. So I got my skateboard and put the box on top of it.

"Now we can roll the box around more easily," I said.

"Are you telling me that the skateboard is a machine?" Peter asked.

"The skateboard has wheels with axles. A wheel and axle is a simple machine. The axle is a rod that goes through the wheel. The axle allows the wheel to roll in place. And because the wheel is round, it doesn't take much force to move it."

"What's force?" asked Peter. "Like Dad's forcing us to do jobs instead of play with George?"

"A force is a push or a pull," I said. "Force is how an object can be put into motion." I made a note in my science notebook.

Big, heavy objects take more force to move than small, light objects. You can push a toy car much more easily than a real car!

Peter pushed the skateboard faster to make George follow it.

Crunch!

"Uh-oh," Peter said.

I thought about it. "The pointed nose of the skateboard is a wedge. That's a kind of simple machine too. A wedge is two slanting planes joined together to make a point. The point is used to split things apart."

"Why would anybody want a simple machine that breaks things?" Peter asked.

"Well," I said, "an axe is a wedge, which can be useful if you need to chop something. A knife is also a wedge. It's great for cutting sandwiches!"

Peter looked at the crack in the wall. "This wedge was definitely not useful in a good way," he said.

"Miaow!" agreed George.

"Let's try to think of some other ways wedges can be used," I said. I wrote them down in my science notebook.

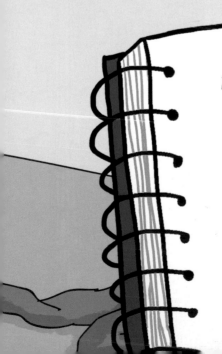

A wedge can be used to separate things, such as a spade breaking up soil. But it can also be used to hold things together or in place. A nail is a wedge that can be used to hold two boards together.

"Hey," Peter said. "Speaking of sandwiches, let's have a snack."

"First, we have to take out the rubbish," I said.

Peter grabbed the bin bag, and we walked outside and down the ramp to the bin.

"This ramp is actually a simple machine," I said.

"One of the simplest. It's an inclined plane. That's a flat surface that is slanted so it's easier to go up and down."

"I get it," Peter said. "It would be hard to jump from up there to the ground. The inclined plane does help."

Back in the kitchen, I grabbed the bread. "Let's make that snack," I said.

Peter twisted the lid off the peanut butter, and that reminded me of something cool.

"Eureka!" I said. "Did you know that this lid is a simple machine? It's called a screw."

"I know what a screw is," Peter said, "and that is not a screw."

"Yes it is," I said. "A screw is a narrow inclined plane that is wrapped around something round. This screw makes a lid that keeps the peanut butter from spilling. It also keeps it fresh." I drew a picture in my notebook to show him how it works.

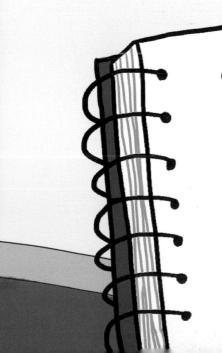

Screws can come in different forms. A screw can go into a wall or board, or it can be the lid of a jar. The lid's groove, or plane, twists onto the jar.

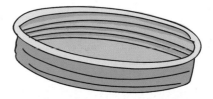

Peter bit into his sandwich. "So, every simple machine is a tool that has a special purpose?" Peter asked.

"Exactly!" I said.

I wanted to show Peter the last two simple machines. One is a pulley. It's a string or rope and a wheel. When you pull on one end, it lifts up the other end. I tied a string to a bucket and used a rolling pin as the wheel.

"Cool!" said Peter. "The wheel helps lift things."

The other simple machine is a lever. A lever is a bar that balances on a base called a fulcrum.

When you use a lever, you apply force to one end. That force moves in the opposite direction on the other end.

"The see-saw we play on at the park is a lever," I told Peter. "You would never be able to lift me that high in the air without the help of a lever!"

"No way!" said Peter as we giggled.

"Our last job is to feed George. Are you ready for some real fun with simple machines?"

"Totally," said Peter.

Peter and I made a plan to use some of the simple machines to feed George. We made an inclined plane out of the lid to his toy box.

We made another inclined plane out of a folder.

"Let's use this ball and racetrack!" Peter said.

"Great idea." I said.

We also made
a lever out of a
metre stick. And the
coolest part of all
was the pulley.

"Eureka!" I said. "We've made a complex
machine!" I opened up my science notebook.

A complex machine is made up
of two or more simple machines
that work together.

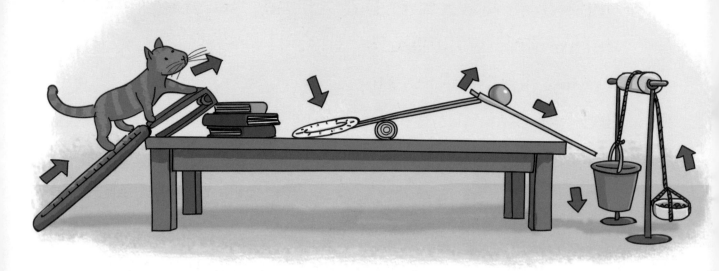

"Let's see if we can predict what will happen with all of these simple machines," I said.

"Why would we want to do that?" Peter asked.

"The whole reason simple machines are helpful is because they change the strength or direction of a force," I said. "But they're only really useful if you know what's going to happen so you can use those forces. So, we look at the machine and try to explain what is going to happen."

We went through all the machines we'd set up. The inclined planes will help George walk up to the top of the machine where the lever is.

When he pushes down on one end of the lever, his downward force will be changed into an upward force.

That will nudge the ball onto another inclined plane. When the ball goes onto the inclined plane, it rolls down and gains speed.

And when the ball rolls into the bucket on one side of the pulley, the other side goes up – bingo! Dinner time.

"Let's see if it works," Peter said.

First, we showed George his mouse toy. He
followed it up the lid and onto the table.

"So far, so good," said Peter.

Then we kept leading him right to the end of the
books and onto the lever. Boing! The cat and the
lever went down, and the other end popped up.
There goes the ball down the inclined plane.

"Super cool!" I said.

The ball went into the bucket. Because it was
heavier than the food, it had more downward force
than the food. So the bucket went down to the
floor, and the food came up.

"Just like we planned it," Peter said.

We gave each other high-fives as George happily
ate his dinner.

"What's going on in here?"

Uh-oh. It was Dad.

"We were just finishing our jobs," I said.

"Your first job was supposed to be tidying up this room – not making a new mess!" said Dad.

"Sorry," Peter said. "We were making simple machines."

"Well, now you have a simple new job," Dad said. "Clear up these machines."

Make a catapult

Are you ready to make your very own simple machine? Build this easy catapult and start experimenting!

Here's what you need:

- A metre stick
- Something to be the fulcrum, such as a log, stack of books or a ball
- A shallow plastic cup
- 1 or more ping-pong balls
- Strong tape
- Optional: a tape measure and pen and paper to record results

Steps:

1. Tape the cup onto the end of the metre stick.

2. In an open area (outside or in a gym), set up your catapult by laying the metre stick over your fulcrum.

3. Put the ping-pong ball in the cup, and push down hard on the other end of the catapult with your hand or foot.

Try putting the fulcrum at different places and pressing the lever harder and softer. What combination makes the ball fly the furthest? What makes it go highest?

GLOSSARY

axle pin or rod on which a wheel turns

force push or pull that moves something

fulcrum pivot or support on which a lever hinges

inclined plane flat surface that is higher on one end so that things can more easily move up or down

lever bar or beam fixed over a fulcrum and used to lift something by applying force to the opposite end

pulley wheel on an axle with a rope or cable that goes around it; pulling down on one end of the rope lifts the other end higher

screw long, narrow inclined plane wrapped around something round and used to fasten two things together

wedge two inclined planes tapered together into a triangular shape and used to separate two objects

READ MORE

How Machines Work, David Macaulay (DK Children, 2015)

Making Machines with Pulleys (Simple Machine Projects), Chris Oxlade (Raintree, 2016)

Simple Machines (Engage Literacy), Kelly Gaffney (Raintree, 2017)

WEBSITE

www.dkfindout.com/uk/science/simple-machines
Find out more about simple machines.

COMPREHENSION ACTIVITIES

You may be surprised how common simple machines are. Make a list of all the simple machines you have used today. How about this week?

Explain why it's helpful to be able to change the strength or direction of a force.

Using two or more simple machines, invent a fun way to do a job or task.

BOOKS IN THIS SERIES

INDEX

axles 5, 7
complex machines 15
forces 7, 13, 16, 17, 19
fulcrums 12
inclined planes 5, 10, 11, 14, 17, 18
levers 5, 12, 13, 15, 17, 18
lifting 12
motions 7
nails 9
pulleys 5, 12, 15, 17
pulls 7, 12
pushes 7, 8, 17
ramps 10
screws 5, 11
see-saws 13
skateboards 6, 7, 8
wedges 5, 8, 9
wheels 5, 7, 12

Thanks to our advisor for his expertise, research and advice: Paul Ohmann, PhD.

Raintree is an imprint of Capstone Global Library Limited, a company incorporated in England and Wales having its registered office at 264 Banbury Road, Oxford, OX2 7DY – Registered company number: 6695582

www.raintree.co.uk
myorders@raintree.co.uk

Designed by Ted Williams and Nathan Gassman
Cover illustrated by Stephanie Dehennin
The illustrations in the book were digitally produced
Original illustrations © Capstone Global Library Limited 2019
Production by Tori Abraham
Originated by Capstone Global Library Ltd
Printed and bound in India

ISBN 978 1 4747 6323 3
22 21 20 19 18
10 9 8 7 6 5 4 3 2 1

British Library Cataloguing in Publication Data
A full catalogue record for this book is available from the British Library.

CURIOUS PEARL

SCIENCE GIRL

CURIOUS PEARL
TINKERS WITH
SIMPLE MACHINES

by Eric Braun
illustrated by Anthony Lewis

shers for children

Curious Pearl here!
Do you like science?

I certainly do! I have all sorts of fun tools to help me observe and investigate, but my favourite tool is my science notebook. That's where I write down questions and facts that help me learn more about science. Would you like to join me on my science adventures? You're in for a special surprise!

CURIOUS PEARL

SCIENCE GIRL